"Golf is deceptively simple and endlessly complicated; it satisfies the soul and frustrates the intellect. It is at the same time rewarding and maddening - and it is without a doubt the greatest game mankind has ever invented."

~Arnold Palmer

Disclaimer

A physician's approval is recommended before beginning any exercise program. The recommendations in this manual are for educational purposes only, they are not medical guidelines. You should consult your physician prior to starting this program or if you have any medical condition or injury that contraindicates physical activity. This program is designed for 18 years, and older individuals deemed healthy.

The information in this manual is meant to supplement, not replace, proper exercise training or dietary regimen that may have been prescribed by your physician. All forms of exercise pose some inherent risk. The authors advise readers to take full responsibility for their safety and know their limits. Before practicing the exercises in this manual, be sure your equipment is well-maintained, and do not take risks beyond your level of experience, aptitude, training, or fitness.

If you are taking any medications, it is recommended to inform your physician before starting any exercise program. If you experience any lightheadedness, dizziness, or shortness of breath while exercising, stop the movement and call your physician.

It is recommended to have a complete physical examination prior to starting this or any new exercise routine if you are sedentary, have high cholesterol, high blood pressure, diabetes, or are overweight.

Copyright Statement

For any use beyond what is allowed by fair use (Title 17, § 107 U.S.C.), you may not reproduce, republish, post, transmit or distribute any portion of this manual in any physical or digital form without the written permission of the copyright owner of the Material.

To purchase a copyright license please contact us at drvcatt@outlook.com

The purpose of this manual is to provide golfers with the knowledge, resources, and guidelines necessary to enhance and improve performance in their golf game. This will be a comprehensive guide to all aspects of health and fitness, which are directly related to golfing.

Important:

This program could involve a specific progression of muscular overload, which involves unstable and dynamic training. A proper warm-up is essential at the beginning of every workout. Although exercising is beneficial, there is a potential for injury involved. Pain & Injury Solutions Inc., Dr. Vince Catteruccia, owners, and employees will not be held liable for injuries sustained while exercising at a gym or elsewhere. Always consult your physician before beginning any exercise program. If you feel any strain, pain, or discomfort while you are exercising, stop immediately and consult your physician.

3

INDEX

A Word from the Author _____ 7

Fundamental Issues _____ 12

Keys to 'Golf Success' _____ 19

Using the Brace in Life _____ 32

Root Yourself _____ 36

Building Root Strength _____ 48

Do the Good Work _____ 58

Using Unstable Surfaces _____ 65

Thank You _____ 71

Contact Dr. Vince _____ 74

A WORD FROM THE AUTHOR

People often ask me if I work with sport-specific athletes, football, soccer, golf, etc. The question strikes me as ironic because my first thought is, of course, I do... I work with the human body. The way I see it, if the body is strong and filled with endurance it doesn't matter what you use it for. At the end of the day, the body should handle whatever you need it to do. Unfortunately for many people, their bodies are not maintained and over time the capacity to perform becomes diminished. In fact, many activities of daily living and hobbies become risky because the body is deconditioned.

Recently, I have been asked to dive into a specific sport because there is a segment of this sport that is in dire need of a reboot. If you're reading this book, then you know how big golf is in your community and you also know the frustrations that come with the sport. If you are lucky the biggest frustration is perfecting your swing but, for many that issue is compounded by a body that hurts before, during, or after you play. Golf is a rather ignominious sport in that it looks simple enough, little white ball, club – swing the club, hit the ball, repeat... But golf requires an insane amount of body control coupled with mental and physical endurance. You cannot just decide to go play golf and think you will enjoy the sport. Nope. In fact, I would argue that golf is one of the hardest sports in that it demands a high level of fitness and emotional intelligence. My goal for you in this book is to reduce the struggle you are having with the mechanics of the swing. We will be discussing two very important but always overlooked elements of body control that will translate into not only golf but life. For many, you could say this will change your Golf Life. Enjoy the a-ha moments you are about to receive.

Nuggets

Old-school ideals maintain that ball flight is primarily controlled by 5 factors: (1) *Club Face Alignment*, (2) *Swing Path*, (3) *Angle of Attack*, (4) *Hitting the Sweet Spot*, (5) *Clubhead Speed*. Swing faults can be expected when a golfer exhibits a weakness in one or more of these factors. A golf pro may notice a number of these weaknesses when viewing a golfer and prescribe certain adjustments to their swing to correct them. Modifications to the stance, swing amplitude, hip/shoulder turn ratio, grip, and so on may be made. Most always, though, these swing alterations are made to compensate for an underlying musculoskeletal issue. Essentially, this is only a way of masking faults or tricking the system, not a way of correcting the problem.

The more compensation a player attempts via alterations to the swing to overcome a structural, musculoskeletal imbalance, the more likely they are to experience inconsistencies in their game. Simply stated, many golfers experience swing limitations due to a lack of body control, muscular imbalances, or weaknesses. However, most golfers focus more on modifying their swing to overcome these limitations rather than working to correct and rid themselves of their muscular imbalances or weaknesses. Therefore, improving body control, balance, and strength of the musculoskeletal system is the most important and effective means of improving your game.

Control the body and the swing will just happen...

Taking a brief deep dive into the world of biomechanics will help you understand why you might not want to splice the golf swing into little bits in an attempt to perfect it. The human movement system is a complicated and mysterious phenomenon that most often runs without thought. If you want to throw a ball, you just do it. You don't stop and think about every piece of the activity and if you do, throwing a ball becomes very arduous. The system responsible for your ability to throw, swing, or jump is the neuromechanical system. This system is a complex of interrelated systems used to perform the golf swing. This is made up of the nervous, muscular, and skeletal systems. Within the neuromechanical system, there are physical factors that dictate the system's state of readiness and ability.

Factors that Influence Golf Readiness & Ability

1. Muscle balance and flexibility (The muscles are of equal size, strength, and tension on both sides of the body)
2. Static and dynamic postural stability (balance and special awareness with or without movement)
3. Strength (amount of force exerted)
4. Power (amount of force exerted over a given distance)

As you can see this is very complex and very few of us have the time or desire to learn the physiology or biomechanics of the golf swing. Lucky for you, all of this is innately held in your ability to understand, practice, and become proficient at controlling two simple parts of the body. To truly learn these two elements, a person must practice enough [through their day's activities] for this to become reflexive or subcortical. When this happens, magic happens. Distance, control, and consistency are no longer your golf quandary. Once you learn this new method of body control, the hardest thing you will do is build endurance and play more golf.

Yes, it is true, each person has a given level of ability and a specific level of skill relative to the demands of golf. Producing a proper swing is not easy. And yes, if a person wants to achieve the highest potential performance it is essential to enhance the physical factors mentioned above. We will address all 5 factors in Volume 2 of this book. For now, let's focus on the most important elements of perfecting your golf swing.

Nuggets

Nuggets

KEYS TO GOLF SUCCESS

One of the biggest mistakes I have seen golfers make is overthinking all of the mechanics involved in hitting the ball much less controlling where the ball ends up. What I'm about to discuss will seem counterintuitive to what you've learned through the years. You've been taught to address the ball a certain way – relax, breathe..., and let the club do its thing. Sounds great but how's that working for you? My guess is you're inconsistent and hoping for the unicorn stroke to happen every time you go out. Your enjoyment in golf shouldn't be measured by the number of times you hit the ball correctly or should I say the least number of times you hit the ball correctly. You should expect to hit the ball the same way every time, consistently. Why is that so hard? It's hard because for many, the focus is spent on buying the current club technology and splicing your swing mechanics into pieces. Then, you're supposed to somehow meld the pieces together over years of practice. One thing is for sure, with this methodology golf will be a lifelong frustration. But this doesn't have to be the case. Golf is about to become a lot more fun…

The Simple Secret

I'd like to frame the rest of this book by explaining exactly where this knowledge impacts your game. The following information has to do with how you set up for or address the ball. Before you swing, there is a sequence of body preparedness you must consider, enhancing everything that happens before you hit the ball. The secret to fun and proficient golf is in your ability to create postural muscle "STIFFNESS" and being able to modulate the intensity during the swing. The other ingredient to Golf Swing Perfection is taking that stiffness and rooting it into the turf. Together these two elements will change your Golf Life forever!

I'll say it again, learning this stiffness and how to root yourself, you will find your Golf Life will be changed forever. Take these two elements and attach the new body awareness to your current golf swing then, forget worrying about *Clubface alignment, Swing Path, Angle of Attack, Hitting the Sweet Spot, and Clubhead Speed.* Of course, it is necessary to train your body to endure the physical demands of the sport and practice regularly to improve ball flight control but now you will be playing golf with a different primary focus.

Funnel the Force

Let's begin with the end in mind. The goal is to create a flow of energy through your body that is efficient at directing the force where you want it to go. For this to happen, you need to become proficient at activating and managing the abdominal brace. Abdominal Bracing is a muscular maneuver where the muscles surrounding the trunk are voluntarily [eventually reflexively] activated. The abdominal brace is the 'funnel' for forces coming from the ground and ending up in the club head.

Let's digress momentarily as I explain how I see a typical golfer addressing the ball.

Photo A demonstrates a golfer that is classically just setting up for a ball without thinking about the brace or rooting. The red line is where the forces stop as they come up from the ground. In this case, the golfer must recreate the forces in their upper body which is why a person fatigues as the round ensues. **Photo B** shows how the forces flow from the ground to the club head when the brace and rooting are active.

A.   B.

In most cases a person sets up (addresses the ball) with a mindset of lining up to the ball, relaxing their body (deep breath), running through a quick checklist of posture (foot position, hands, head, etc.), and then a quick prayer that all things align… Looking at photo A, this person is praying the ball goes where he wants it to go. Notice the red line through the hips. This depicts the rubber wall that the forces (created in the legs) hit as he runs through the stroke mechanics. The setup is wrong… From the way he sets up to his follow-through, it's wrong. If the abdominal brace is off and there is no rooting into the ground, the ball strike is a guess. In this scenario, the force (the power) must be recreated above the red line. Essentially the power of the golfer is reduced significantly, and the swing becomes very inefficient. Notice the fluid green line in photo B. This depicts the power flowing through the "Force Funnel" that naturally occurs when the deep root stabilizers (the brace) are active. In other words, the power flows through the abdominal brace up into the torso, arms, and ultimately into the club head. Whammo!

The ball strike sounds amazing. The ball flight is perfect. Every time!

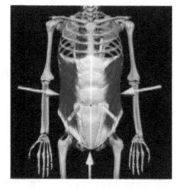

The overall stability that the bracing technique creates around the lower spine is invaluable in terms of swing efficiency and reproducible accuracy. Stability is a joint's capacity to maintain proper alignment under load during movement. It [stability] is a joint's ability to resist internal and external forces. For the lower (lumbar) spine, this is related to how effectively the abdominal muscles can create and maintain (endure) an isometric contraction. It is this isometric contraction that creates resistance to movement, protecting the spine from external forces.

The first thing you need to learn is how to properly activate and maintain abdominal activity during daily life. The most effective way to do this is to simply learn how to perform an isometric contraction of the deep abdominal muscles. This is known as an abdominal brace. This brace will increase stiffness, and stability throughout the lumbar spine as well as set the pelvis in its natural neutral position. Ultimately setting the lower spine and pelvis to handle the generation of forces coming up from the ground, through the body, and into the hands (golf club).

Once you have learned to activate and manage this brace throughout your day, challenges can be added that will increase your endurance and strength. For instance, planks, dead bugs, floor bridges, and side planks. For now, the goal is to learn control of the abdominal brace in conjunction with just breathing.

Remember, it's not just about being able to contract the abdominal muscles. You also need to be able to maintain the brace during golf and daily activities.

In the early stages of learning the bracing technique, it's normal for a person to find it very difficult to maintain deep abdominal activity and breathe normally. The contraction is often lost as you inhale. This is a challenge that needs to be overcome with consistent practice. Abdominal activation needs to be independent of respiration. Otherwise, you will not realize the value of the brace and your lower spine will remain unstable, unable to funnel forces, and susceptible to injury.

Here's how to perform the

basic Abdominal Brace:

1. Begin on your back in a relaxed neutral spine position

2. Gently contract your abdominal muscles. It is often helpful to imagine you are about to be hit in the stomach and you need to tense your abdominal muscles for protection.

3. Now try to hold the abdominal contraction as you breathe in and out.

4. Remember the abdominal tension is out not in.

Note: It can be helpful in the initial stages to press your fingertips into the line between your abdominal and oblique muscles to feel the muscle activity. You are not trying to activate or tighten the "6-pack abs" you are feeling the tension in the side wall of the abdominal region. Once you have this figured out, the contraction/stiffness of the abdominal muscles should remain steady (the same) during each breath. Repeat this process throughout the day.

Keynote: During the day, walking about, you should have 30% tension in the abdominal brace muscles. When pulling a heavy door open, getting in and out of your car, lifting groceries, etc. you will increase the activity in the brace to match the demand. For instance, pulling a heavy door open you will need 60-70% brace tension. Whereas, carrying a 50# bag of softener salt downstairs requires 100% abdominal bracing tension.

Nuggets

Nuggets

.

Mastering the abdominal brace requires that you are using it in all of life's movements. *Abdominal Bracing is not just for an isolated workout each day.* As I said, this bracing technique needs to be used to pull open doors, get in and out of your car, etc... <u>From this moment on you are responsible for the control of the Abdominal Brace at all times in the day.</u> You will know when you're being lazy because you will feel low back discomfort again or you will feel 'less' strong and you will fatigue quickly.

Abdominal Brace = Swing Efficiency

Abdominal Brace = Ball Flight Control

Abdominal Brace = No Pain

As I mentioned before, muscle balance and static/dynamic postural stability are intimately related to control of all swing mechanics and ball flight factors. That said, without the activity and control of the abdominal brace, strength, and balance mean nothing in the sport of Golf. To say this in another way, working toward increasing club head speed will be futile without owning the abdominal brace. This is important to know because, most golfers who take part in a training program spend most of their time developing the physical factors hoping to improve clubhead speed and ball flight, but they are missing the reflexive, deep-root muscular control that underlies every aspect of this goal.

Nuggets

You got it! You understand the abdominal brace technique. Now you're ready to get after it!

Not so fast...

I love that you understand the brace... but there is another very crucial piece to perfecting your swing. We need to take this amazing, strong stable body and firmly stick it into the ground. In 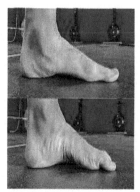 various forms of martial arts, it is known that your ability to produce and control power is derived from the ground. It's often said in Tai Chi that your feet need to grip the ground. This is achieved by slightly raising the arch of the foot, so the feet create a fist-like action that affords you improved stability, balance, and grip. The question is, how do you do it?

It doesn't sound very relaxed to 'grip' the ground with your feet.

On the contrary, in fact, the arch of the foot and the grip of the toes is achieved through softness, rather than hardness. The answer is found in what is called "the wrapping of the legs".

If you point your knees outwards slightly you create a kind of gentle wrapping in the legs as you move, and, if you let it, this wrapping will encourage the toes to grip the ground and the foot arch to form. Of course, it should be emphasized that the action of the knee pointing outwards is achieved not by pointing the knee itself, but by rounding the inner thigh area. Another way of looking at this would be to screw your feet, gently, into the ground as if you were twisting the ground outward with your foot sole. Keyword, gently.

Deep Dive into Rooting

The gripping action of the feet gives

you better than normal balance,

especially in sports or fighting

postures. If you've ever looked at a Tai Chi practitioner

standing on one leg without wobbling and wondered how they

do it. The key is their knee as it's being <u>gently</u> pointed

outwards. The operative word is gentle, if you are making this

all happen using too much tension, then you might end up

causing more harm than good, so beware of the finesse

required in this new skill set. None of the postural

considerations I mention should be achieved through tensing

parts of the body. That's the key. You need to walk the middle

way between trying to make something happen too hard and

not trying hard enough. That's the enigma of the rooting

strategy and the reason for perfect practice.

A strength perspective on rooting

Rooting in the world of golf is just that, *anchoring your body to the ground*...LOCKING the body into the turf. Much like hands gripping a bar, the feet need to grip the ground if you're going to create optimal stability and generate maximal power.

For the engineering mind; What Rooting Does:

1. Increases Surface Area
   a. The larger the surface area the more stable the base.
   b. "A pyramid is only as tall as its base is wide"
   c. The more surface area you can push through and the more locked into the ground you can be, the more power you'll generate.

2. Activates the Foot
   a. The feet are our initial point of sensory feedback from the ground.
   b. Pressure, load, compression, angles, etc. on the foot tell the brain and rest of the body a lot about the environment and how to compensate.

  c. An active foot tells the rest of the body to get prepared, lock-in, and generate power.

 3. Activates the Glutes: The Powerhouse

   a. Your glutes are important for optimal performance and power.

   b. Your big toe is key to the activity of the glutes.

The Short Foot Method

Rooting into the floor is done through the creation of what has been termed a "short foot". The concept is simple, there are three primary points of foot contact to focus on.

3 The Big Toe

2 The Little Toe

1 The Whole heel

Done correctly, there should be pressure on all three aspects of the short foot. Sometimes you hear, "Equal pressure on each area". But not really. It's usually more like:

Big Toe: 30%

Little Toe: 20%

Heel: 50%

The point is, if you distribute your weight through these three areas, you'll have pressure across the foot more evenly distributed and you'll have more surface area to generate power from.

The "short foot" is about foot activation, creating tension through the foot. This is mostly done through gentle cinching or shortening of the arch, it's not curling your toes.

If you have foot pronation, otherwise known as fallen arches, you will have a very hard time generating any power. Pronation of the feet inhibits the activity of the gluteal muscles, namely the gluteus

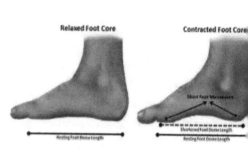

Relaxed Foot Core   Contracted Foot Core

maximus muscle. The glute max is your powerhouse. You were most likely not born with a fallen arch. The arch can fatigue over time.

That said, we all should, to varying degrees, be able to grip the ground with our feet (tighten up our arch). When you do this, it's about creating gentle tension in the foot. If you're trying to do this and you're like, "yeah, that did nothing". It's because you're doing it wrong. I would bet that you're not gripping the ground, not putting force into the ground.

If you're trying to "grip the ground" and not getting tension in the arch you're most likely just curling your toes. Curling your toes puts zero force in the ground. Remember, rooting is about locking yourself into the ground, pulling the energy from the ground through the feet, up into the whole body. Simply sliding your toes back, and curling them up, will shorten your arch, but it's because your foot is being curled up. Not because it's creating active tension. Much like if you ball your hand up in a fist vs. gripping a barbell. If you're crushing something in your hand, you're going to create a lot more force and stiffness through the arm and shoulder than if you just ball your hand up.

You now have two new focal points that need the practice to become engrained as reflexes so that when you are addressing the ball everything sets up without thought. Many will ask, "how long does it take to become reflexive or subcortical"? This is unique to the person. For some, it takes a few short weeks and for others, it takes months of practice. What I can tell you is the more you practice and use these new elements in your daily life the faster you will learn them. What's funny to me is that at one time we all innately actively used the brace and the short foot but, as we age and sit more, we lose these deep stabilizing reflexes.

If you don't use it, you lose it...

Nuggets

Nuggets

"I think that what I've found for me personally

is that this game that we play is a sport. You

must treat it as such. Traditionally, people in

the past never treated it as a sport. Nobody

else would think twice – a football player lifting

a whole bunch of weights to get stronger, a

basketball player, a track and field athlete, a

baseball player, you name it, go right down the

line. It is a sport, and there are certain parts of

the body that you need to have strong and

stable to help you swing the golf club properly

and more consistently. I have enjoyed that

aspect of improving my physical strength."

- Tiger Woods (June 21, 2000)

The aim of this book is to help you become a more efficient and consistent golfer! To achieve this goal, it is critical to become proficient at using the brace and rooting skills. It's also important that you have a minimum level of understanding of posture, balance, stability, endurance, and strength. The following is a brief explanation of each of these facets as they relate to golf.

Posture

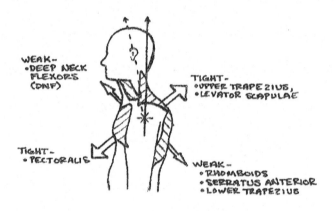

Upper Cross Posture

Posture is the sum of the position of all the joints in the body at any given moment. In today's day and age, the typical posture is forward drawn (aka upper crossed); rounded shoulders, head forward, caved chest and rounded back. Upper Cross posture describes the presentation of the upper body formed from having weak deep neck flexors and weak mid and low traps, combined with tight upper traps and tight pecs. This posture is extremely weak and injury-prone, especially when combined with the torsional stress of the golf swing. Commonly this dysfunctional upper body posture is accompanied by Lower Cross Posture. Lower Cross Posture is formed from having weak abdominals and weak glutes combined with tight spinal erectors and tight hip flexors.

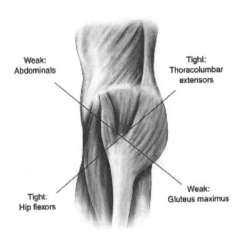

Weak:
Abdominals

Tight:
Thoracolumbar
extensors

Tight:
Hip flexors

Weak:
Gluteus maximus

Lower Cross Posture

The correct posture is shoulders back (slightly retracted), chin tucked slightly, chest up, and abdominals taught (braced). This is a strong and stable posture and will allow for the increased maximum potential of biomechanical angles and force vectors. When carried over to the golf swing, this translates to greater power production. Posture is important both to aid in trunk stability and to protect yourself against injury from the high amount of torsion from the golf swing.

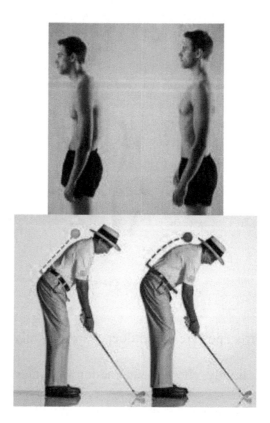

As you can see in the photos above, standing posture or the posture you exhibit daily translates into your golf posture.

Nuggets

Nuggets

Whether you are a weekend golfer or you're chasing

trophies, you need to practice and train to match the

demands of the sport. In this case, golf is one of the

most demanding. I like to call this sport,

"ignominious" or, unsuspecting in its physical

requirements. Long-distance walking, bending,

squatting, twisting, lunging, all for a long duration...,

Often, unbeknownst to its participant Golf is a sport

requiring a high level of fitness. In this section, my

goal is to define each parameter of Golf so that you

understand the "why" it's so important to prepare for

each round. Obviously, you want to perform well,

consistently improve, enjoy the time and most of all

avoid injury. To do so it is imperative that you are

flexible, full of strong endurance and that you have

control of your body. The following will define each of Golf's critical elements

Flexibility – "A short, tight muscle can do no work." Power generation and flexibility are linked in the sense that if your muscles are shortened to the point of changing your posture, there is no way (unless you compensate *a lot*) that you can generate any substantial amount of power. Also, if muscles are tight, blood flow is impeded. This restricts proper nutrient and oxygen exchange to the muscles. Therefore, breathing can be challenged and the miles of walking necessary during a round of golf will be very taxing. Finally, flexible muscles will allow for a full range of motion, which will allow for complete rotation and greater power production. [A study conducted at Centinela Hospital Medical Center in California showed that the significant difference between professional and amateur golfers was that the amateurs used only half of the hip rotation that the professionals had].

Active stretching prior to a round of golf is beneficial because it will help to release any bonds or adhesions that naturally form while your system was inactive. Releasing "tight" inactive muscles increases elasticity, and the muscle's ability to store and release energy. This then enhances the production of power that is translated into club head speed. So, stretching enhances the ability to preload the muscles and generate power – think of a catapult.

A major benefit of exercising on an unstable surface such as an airex pad or wobble board is its ability to help improve the endurance of deep stabilizers and improve flexibility without over-stressing the joints or the muscles. This is partly because by being on an unstable surface, your body uses the smaller stabilizing muscles to balance itself while at the same time turning off the larger muscle groups, the ones that tend to be tightest, allowing them to relax. Exercising on most unstable surfaces constitutes active stretching, stretching muscles while strengthening them as well.

Strength & Endurance

Strength training has three major benefits:

1) It can improve your muscular and cardiovascular endurance.

2) It can improve your overall distance.

3) It is one of the fastest ways to burn fat and lose weight.

Strength training is crucial to any athlete, professional or amateur. Proper strength training programs will increase muscular strength and endurance consecutively which helps golfers perform and feel their best during play, prevent injuries related to the stresses of the golf swing, and allow for increased force potential of the swing. A total golf strength program, like the one described in Volume 2, includes exercising all the primary muscles that assist the golf swing, and deep postural stability. The goal of the strength program is to improve muscular strength, enable the muscles to perform as stabilizers, and train the muscles for maintenance of posture, balance, and weight shifting during rotation throughout the golf swing.

As you know, a round of Golf requires the body to perform for 3-5 hours which means it is very much an endurance sport (like a marathon). If you want to make big improvements, adding a full-body strength training program at least two times a week is imperative. Make sure you focus on full-body routines with at least three sets of 20-25 repetitions per exercise [5-7 exercises per workout is typically a sweet spot]. Taking it a step further, I recommend wearing a heart-rate monitor. A monitor will guide your intensity and rest periods.

We will take a deep dive into the use of heart rate-based training in Volume 2.

"What people lose right off the bat more than anything is their endurance, their muscle and power endurance," Even a casual golfer could take between 200-400 swings per round including practice cuts and swings on the range. *"If your body is not prepared to deal with that level of endurance and it doesn't have the durability, compensation will occur, bad habits will occur, and sometimes even injury."* – Dr. Vince

Nuggets

Nuggets

USING UNSTABLE SURFACES TO ENHANCE GOLF

PERFECTION

Proximal stability = distal mobility. Stability and balance

go hand in hand, and both are critical in a high-velocity

rotational movement such as the golf swing. Together,

stability and balance allow for a reflex that maintains balance

during a shift in the center of gravity. Structural stability

comes from a strong "core" and the ability to control it on

demand. Your "core" is a group of muscles that includes the

abdominals, lower back, and gluteals. Combined these

muscles form the foundation from which all movement

originates. The core is the center of postural endurance – in

other words, the ability to maintain core stability and control

over time. Maintaining core stability will allow you to lock

down your ribcage and pelvis so that the power generated in

the hips isn't lost before it reaches the club head (aka

abdominal bracing).

Working on unstable surfaces effectively strengthens your core musculature. These muscles help the trunk maintain position while other parts are moving. "Proximal stability = distal mobility." Having a stable base (hips and torso) permits you to move your extremities (arms and legs) more freely and powerfully, during movements like a golf swing.

- The less intelligent the player, the more certain he is to offer insights into the mental side of the game.

Weight Shifting – Whenever you lay down, stand, sit, or put your feet on an unstable surface, the body automatically activates and integrates reflexes (reactions to right yourself, providing equilibrium). Using an unstable surface enhances reflexes during golf, which is important due to the need for a powerful weight shift from the back leg to the front leg during the backswing through to the downswing. If this weight shift is inhibited due to a lack of these reflexes, all speed, power, and control will be severely limited.

Balance – Unstable surface exercises make it necessary for the whole body to participate in the effort to maintain correct posture while trying to stay in balance. Over time, this greatly improves overall balance, without good balance, golfers tend to lean or fall forward while reaching with the club to hit the ball or during the follow-through.

"Whatever you think you're doing wrong is probably

the one thing you're doing right." -anonymous

Nuggets

Nuggets

THANK YOU

It's my pleasure to share my knowledge of human movement and biomechanics. As you may have gleaned from this short book, this [Golf] is a complex conversation. One that if you break it into too many parts can be overwhelming. Therefore, my goal was to deliver this information in a short concise manner. If you would like to see this information in more detail, presented to a group or in a personal setting, please do not hesitate to reach out to me.

Remember, it's not necessarily your golf club or the swing itself..., it could be how you control your posture and the endurance of your posture that is your conundrum.

One last thing. You might wonder if I'm a golfer. Sure, I was. From the age of 4 until I was 30, then my profession took me away from this sport because of time. So, yes. I understand golf and all its challenges. Do I work with

Golfers? Yes. But I would like to elaborate on this by saying I am an expert in human movement therefore I work with the body that is used to play golf. The goal for that body is to be powerful and injury-free for life.

Dr. Vince Catteruccia is an internationally known Musculoskeletal Diagnostician, Author, and Founder of Workforce Intelligence who is recognized for uncovering hidden sources of physical pain and producing lasting solutions for his patients — without medication or surgery. His natural approach to solving  pain is guided by his unique combination of professional credentials including a Ph.D. in Behavior, a Master's of Science in Kinesiotherapy, and a Master's of Science in Human Performance.

He's learned from the best in the world, traveling the globe to uncover natural solutions to nagging pain including time in Prague at the renowned Motol Hospital of Rehabilitation and Manual Medicine. During his 30-year career, Dr. Vince is proud to have helped thousands of people end their battles with chronic pain. Today, he lives in Arizona with his wife, Jennifer, and his son, Gabriel, where he works with patients worldwide virtually and in person.

Dr. Vincent R. Catteruccia

www.drvincecatteruccia.com

Call/Text 480.462.9894

Please look for my other books on Amazon & Audible

Damned by the Diagnosis

A Different Way of Thinking About Pain

What's Next?

Fitness & Life...Now!

Igniting Change & Impact in Health,

Made in the USA
Monee, IL
09 February 2023

26574764R00046